I Want Those Shoes

I Want Those Shoes

Paola Jacobbi

Translated by Simonetta Wenkert

Illustrated by Emma Farrarons

BLOOMSBURY

First published 2004 as Voglio quelle scarpe!

Copyright © 2004 Sperling & Kupfer Editori

Translation copyright © 2006 by Simonetta Wenkert
Illustrations copyright © 2006 by Emma Farrarons

The moral right of the author has been asserted

Bloomsbury Publishing Plc
36 Soho Square
London WID 3QY

A CIP catalogue record for this book
is available from the British Library

ISBN 0 7475 8246 7

ISBN–13 9780747582465

10 9 8 7 6 5 4 3 2 1

Typeset by Hewer Text UK Ltd, Edinburgh
Printed in Great Britain by Clays Ltd, St lves plc

The paper this book is printed on is certified by the
© Forest Stewardship Council 1996 A.C. (FSC). It is
ancient-forest friendly. The printer holds FSC chain
of custody SGS-COC-2061

FSC

Mixed Sources
Product group from well-managed
forests and other controlled sources

Cert no. SGS-COC-2061
www.fsc.org
© 1996 Forest Stewardship Council

This book is dedicated to women,
who understand. And also to men, who don't.
But who, in the end, grow to appreciate.

The madness of women,
That need for shoes
That will hear no reason.
What do millions matter
When in exchange you have shoes?

Elio e Le Storie Tese,
'La follia della donna'

CONTENTS

Introduction

Five years ago, I moved into my current apartment. The previous tenant, the usual friend-of-a-friend, was a very sporty type, with a decided flair for DIY. Whilst showing me the features of the house, he paused proudly before a recess in the wall, which he had skilfully transformed into a spacious cupboard replete with shelves, where he kept his numerous mountaineering jumpers (he's not the jacket-and-tie sort).

At the sight of this, I was filled with excitement, and cried out, 'How wonderful! That's where I can store my shoes!'

He stared at me in amazement, and asked, 'Well, how many shoes do you own? I myself possess four: two for the winter, and two for the summer!'

If ever I had doubted it, here was the proof: men and women are very different in several respects, but the moment you get on to the subject of shoes, there exists a chasm between the two sexes.

It has been calculated that the average person walks around three thousand kilometres during their lifetime. Thus, while shoes are useful objects for both sexes, it is only for women they become an all-consuming obsession.

Women's magazines tell us how to use shoes to find ourselves a husband, re-conquer a lost lover, or get that job we hanker after.

They can cost a fortune; yet while money itself does not bring happiness, a pair of new shoes can bring about a kind of exaltation that comes pretty close to that fleeting feeling described by the philosophers. The reason is often a mystery. One explanation may be that, unlike many other objects – clothes, for example – shoes have a distinct advantage. Whether you're fat or thin, short or tall, beautiful or ugly, you can buy all the shoes your heart desires.

Shoes possess magical properties: they're capable of making you feel splendid or sexy, elegant or sporty at a single stroke. In spite of the soles coming into contact with less than immaculate streets, and indeed our own sweat, shoes remain works of art – or at least of a kind of noble craftsmanship, which at the end of the day is not that far removed from that of jewellery. With the difference that they cost somewhat less than diamonds, considered to be 'a girl's best friend'. Which in the end is what shoes are: our best friends.

At this point, I have to come clean and admit that the aim of this book is not to arrive at a definitive understanding of the subject, because that would be impossible. The French director François Truffaut maintained that cinema-goers had two professions: their own, as well as that of film critic. In just the same way, all women are experts on shoes.

They always have been, but over the last ten years this phenomenon has increased massively due to several factors. In order to increase the popularity of their brands, the great fashion houses have invested a great deal in the production of accessories: not only shoes, but bags, glasses and cosmetics, all of which are in a far more affordable price range than clothes.

For a long time, the obsession with luxury shoes has been the prerogative of a select caste of It Girls, the females of the international jet set: actresses, socialites, millionairesses: a tribe whose members could be identified by the accessories with which they adorned themselves. Their distinguishing tattoos were the labels: Hermès, Gucci, Caovilla, Ferragamo, Blahnik, which they procured by putting their names down on the special waiting lists of international boutiques.

Subsequently, in accordance with the new commercial politics of the top brands, what was once the preserve of an elite has now been extended to the masses. The brands have multiplied or branched out into numerous diffusion lines, along with their collector-buyers.

Over the last couple of years, producers have

described the state of the shoe market as being critical, as is the case with other fashion sectors: decreasing exports, an increase in imports of mass-produced, shoddier goods from China, Vietnam and India. And yet, in spite of these intimations of economic crisis, or perhaps precisely because of them, a pair of high-quality shoes continues to be seen as a form of intelligent investment, partly due to the philosophy of 'spending more to spend less', partly because a pair of designer shoes is a universal status symbol, and one that is difficult to renounce. For those people unable to afford the hot new pieces of a collection there exist stores, outlets and markets, where at a far lower price one can easily pick up models that certainly haven't yet lost their lustre.

Perhaps, in order for shoes to become once more truly exclusive objects, we will have to return to made-to-measure products, as happened before the Second World War. It's not a coincidence that in London there now exists a two-day shoe-manufacturing course (Prescott & Mackay. For further information see the website, www.prescottandmackay.co.uk).

Frankly, I don't believe that this initiative will be particularly successful. The attraction of shoes rests entirely in the encounter: there they lie, splendid, virginal, on show for all to see in a well-illuminated city-centre shop, or else jumbled up on a pile in a market stall.

A shoe, just like love, can awaken violent instincts. I have seen things that men would never believe possible, but which women have experienced first-hand: fisticuffs for the last pair of leopard skin shoes in a size 37, elbow jabs to get to a ridiculous pair of gold sandals, and even insults exchanged for an absolutely ordinary-looking pair of brown ankle boots – shame that everyone wanted them.

Our passion for shoes has an extraordinary history behind it. Mankind remained barefoot for precious little time. Already, in certain prehistoric drawings, one can make out footwear derived from animal skins. The evolution of shoes proceeded apace alongside fashion and customs.

Finally, here is my own personal 'shoeography'. I wrote the book you now hold between your hands whilst almost exclusively wearing a pair of Nike Pegasus, the same trainers I use for jogging. For me, this is the equivalent of being barefoot.

Whilst wandering around the city in search of inspiration, looking in shop windows and taking special note of the shoes women were walking around in, I was never without my pair of black, medium-heeled, slightly pointed brushed-calfskin boots, which were one of my most successful purchases of the winter 2002–2003. They taught me one thing: what you're looking for is not always on display, even in the better-stocked shops. Carefully explain to the assistant what it is you're after. In the storeroom there might lie – as was the case with my beloved boots – the exact model you're looking for, but which, thanks to the mysterious rules of fashion, might not fit into the trend of the moment.

When I went to interview Sara Porro, one of the best shoe designers around, I made the great mistake of wearing an old pair of Hogan suede lace-up ankle boots (it was freezing cold!). Being a kind of high priestess of elegant footwear, she gave me a filthy look, but she then charmingly forgave me.

On the other hand, for my trip to the Ferragamo Museum in Florence, I wore a pair of Dolce and Gabbana shoes from the 2000 collection in patent leather and snakeskin, with an ankle strap and fairly low heel, which had become quite comfortable through intensive use. This too was a bit of a gaffe, but the best I could do under the circumstances, in view of the intense day I had ahead of me. They too were kind enough not to comment. Thanks for that!

In order to clelebrate the end of this marvellous journey into an obsession – mine and others' – I haven't yet decided which shoes to wear. I might go and buy a new pair for the occasion. In fact, come to think of it, I really need some.

Women Who Talk with their Feet
(and Run on Heels)

The story is told of how certain Neapolitan politicians in the fifties used to present potential voters with the gift of a single shoe: after the vote, they would complete the pair. Indeed, shoes are a perfect metaphor for a couple, as is sadly underlined by the expression adopted by many abandoned women: 'He tossed me aside like an old shoe' – a single shoe being the ultimate in unusable objects. Particularly when there's only one left, at which point there really is no difference between a woman and a shoe.

In Italian, we have the expressions 'to talk with one's feet', 'to write with one's feet' or 'to act with one's feet'. In other words, to do something extremely badly or carelessly, lacking in all goodwill or expertise. This negative connotation derives from the contrast between (noble) hands and (ignoble) feet. It is archaic to see the hands as being nearer to the mind and the heart, while feet remain down below, mere brainless means of transport.

In English, however, it is crystal clear that shoes (and by extension the feet contained within them) are the foundations of the personality of the person who is wearing them. 'Putting oneself in someone's shoes' would be 'wearing someone's clothes' in Italian. As is often the case, the English language is more efficient than the Italian. Think about it: putting oneself in someone's shoes is truly an intimate gesture, far more so than borrowing some clothes.

For women in particular, this is so intimate as to be one of the first things we do after learning to stand up straight. As soon as we want to feel 'grown-up', we slip on a pair of our mother's shoes, preferably high-heeled ones. In so doing, we climb on to a pedestal that instantly heightens our sense of what it is to be female. However fleetingly, those 'stolen' shoes make us grow in every sense of the word.

While psychoanalysts describe this as an act of 'projection', I remember it being a magical moment. All dressing-up games started from this.

For adults, the sight of a little girl in high-heeled shoes is both tender and comical. For the child, however, it marks entry into a world of aspirations and dreams. The sensation of her chubby little legs wandering around in the objects that Mummy herself walks in creates the illusion that soon, she too, will be able to do those 'grown-up' things that due to her age are forbidden to her.

Sigmund Freud would argue that this childish appropriation of the maternal shoes almost constitutes a seduction ploy aimed at the father, a little girl's attempt to assume the mother's role.

And then what happens? You do grow up, you get to be the same size as Mummy, and the personality begins to assert itself with the first individual purchase of shoes. As adults, we ask shoes to be our representatives. The beauty of this is that they needn't permanently define us. At any given moment of our lives, and even of a single day, they are indicators of our age, mood and desires. Shoes say everything about a woman.

The actress, Penelope Cruz, confesses, 'I have never been able to study a new role until the director and I have chosen the shoes that the woman we are about to bring to the screen will be wearing. Everything starts down there.'

Thus, the question remains: what *do* women say when they talk with their feet?

Sex and the Shoe

Women's shoes, more than anything else, talk the language of sex.

You don't have to be a moralist/fetishist like Nanni Moretti (picture the procession of feet in the film, *Bianca*) nor, with respect, the anthropologist Desmond Morris, in order to understand the different messages transmitted by a girl in a pair of silent, rubber-soled moccasins and a girl wearing noisy stilettos. But only at first sight, for that old chestnut (heels = sex goddess, flatties = nun) is constantly challenged by variations in fashion and customs. And yet one thing remains certain: a high-heeled shoe is the one object more than any other that marks out the difference between the male and female of our species.

Just to get things straight: have you ever seen a transsexual in pumps? And, for all the talk about Millennium Man being a Narcissus and a flirt, he's never yet been spotted in a pair of stilettos. They've said yes to mascara on their eyelashes, eyeshadow on their eyelids, and even to the fiendishly painful practice of waxing; but they haven't yet got round to wearing stilettos, at least outside cross-dressing-themed gay parties.

Though, who knows, it might yet happen. For the ever-growing number of 'metrosexual' men, those in other words who are inspired by the fashion proclivities of a figure like David Beckham, that day could come sooner rather than later. Which would signal a period of collective mourning for us women, and would be the subject of an entirely different book. For now, at least, it is out of the question.

Stilettos are girls' stuff. The higher and pointier the heel, the more they are seen as a symbolic declaration of our diversity and therefore the more blatantly provocative. 'Mine are higher than yours,' is what those clickety-clacking women in streets and offices are really saying. Yup, that's their message to women they're competing with; and above all, to the men with whom they're engaged in either love or war.

Surely it's no coincidence either that, from 'Cinderella' onwards, the popular female narrative has been greatly concerned with shoes. Prince Charming is bagged, thanks to a pair, be they the glass slippers (clearly a symbol of virginity) belonging to the chaste Cinderella, or a pair of stilettos worn by the metropolitan predators of *Sex and the City*. In New York, capital of the Western world, four women in their thirties recount their adventures and scrapes in the worlds of sex, work and shopping. Intelligent, active, modern women, who share two great weaknesses: men and shoes.

In this instance, too, shoes are an integral part of their personalities. 'Sometimes, when we're about to shoot a close-up, the director will say to me that I can take off my shoes, seeing as my feet won't be in the frame,' says Sarah Jessica Parker. 'But I've never done it: the expression of a woman in flatties is totally different from one in heels.'

A truth that hasn't escaped Patricia Fields, wardrobe stylist of *Sex and the City*, who has created a new cult out of the dazzling designer shoes and clothes worn by the women in the show.

The cream of the crop, insofar as the shoes are concerned, are undoubtedly the Manolo Blahniks – a brand that is to shoes what Ferrari is to luxury cars. In one episode, Carrie (Sarah Jessica Parker) gets lost, and ends up in an alleyway, face to face with a mugger. She begs him, 'take my bag, my ring, my watch, but leave me my Manolos!' A paradoxical one-liner that hints at a new scale of values. Which is probably why it has become so well known, at least among *Sex and the City* aficionados.

In another episode, Carrie attends a baby shower. Seeing as it's an informal occasion, the hostess asks the guests to remove their shoes on entering the hallway. At the end of the afternoon, Carrie can't find her Manolos: they've been nicked by a modern-day magpie, attracted by their beauty and sparkle.

Having shoes as the protagonists of such a popular TV show has transformed a secret label for a few privileged fashion insiders into a mass myth – at least insofar as its followers are concerned: you can't buy a pair of Manolos for less than $400!

The Blahnik brand has even penetrated the world of rap music. In Jay-Z's song, 'Bonnie and Clyde', dedicated to his pop-star girlfriend Beyonce Knowles, the rap artist promises to love and cherish his woman by offering her a Hermès Birkin bag, a Mercedes Benz, and a pair of Manolos.

Manolo Blahnik was born in the Canary Islands in 1941. After studying Fine Art and Architecture, he moved to New York in the early seventies, where he met Diana Vreeland, the legendary editor of *Vogue*, who encouraged him to design shoes. His first devotees were the most glamorous actresses of the age: Marisa Berenson, Jane Birkin, Charlotte Rampling. Today, his shoes can be found not only in high-class boutiques, and on the feet of the likes of Kate Moss and Jennifer Aniston, but also in design museums.

Manolo's comment on the lengths people will go to for a pair of his shoes, and for shoes in general, is, 'Women love transforming themselves, and shoes are the quickest and easiest way for them to achieve instant metamorphosis. And they cost less than a piece of jewellery, or an haute-couture frock.'

Another high-profile brand of sexy shoes that has come to the fore in recent years is Jimmy Choo. So much so, that in British bingo halls the number thirty-two is now made to rhyme with Jimmy Choo. Tamara Mellon, the owner of the company that can count actresses such as Halle Berry and Catherine Zeta Jones among its devotees, declared, 'The amazing popularity of accessories in recent years can easily be explained. People these days dress in a way that's increasingly unstructured and casual. Bags and above all shoes are all that remain to add a sexy touch to a person's look.'

In Italy, one of the great producers of shoes that are both sexy and, according to those in the know, comfortable is Sergio Rossi, now part of the Gucci group. One of the most skilful artisans specialising in 'precious' shoes is René Fernando Caovilla, who happens to be a Venetian, in spite of his bullfighter's name. His creations almost exclusively sport vertiginously high heels, are highly decorative, and very, very sexy.

Caovilla says, 'I don't make shoes to be worn every day to the office: they are prized objects that celebrate female beauty.' They are erotic artefacts, worn in order to be discarded at the threshold of the bedroom. And in fact a pair of luxury stilettos is the stuff of fetishists' dreams, as testified by the proliferation of porn websites dedicated to female extremities.

It was Freud who drew our attention to the fact that the foot is a full-blown erogenous zone, complete with highly sensitive nerve-endings, and that fetishism is not so much a perversion as one element of an erotic relationship, in which the object is substituted for the person. Fetishism is an extreme fantasy, at times an indicator of an incomplete sexuality. As Karl Kraus put it, in one of his memorable aphorisms, 'There is no more unhappy being than a fetishist who yearns for a female shoe, and has to make do with the complete woman.' At other times, however, fetishism is merely one of many innocent seduction games in which the man watches and the woman acts, walking on her heels, whilst putting herself through exquisite torture.

Like the heroic Italian soubrette Simona Ventura, who spent five hours of live coverage of the Sanremo Music Festival perched on a pair of sparkly sandals with murderous twelve-centimetre heels. At the end of this tour de force, the poor creature muttered to her pan-European audience, 'My feet are like a pair of sausages.'

The Comfortable Moccasin

In Spain, the gossips of the *prensa del corazon* recount how Letizia Ortiz, the television journalist and their future queen, never used to wear heels before she met Prince Felipe. From that day onwards, she never wore anything less than nine centimetres in order to reach the height of His Highness. Before, however, Letizia would often be seen wearing moccasins. This is because moccasins are comfortable shoes, par excellence – the footwear of choice for the woman who has her head screwed on, and plenty to get done. For the woman who drives, who is into sport, and who has no time for frivolous pursuits. However, above all, they are for middle-class women who have grown up in circles where the very sight of a high-heeled shoe is considered to be 'vulgar', and where even the most oblique reference to sex is kept quiet for the sake of discretion.

And what could be more discreet than a pair of moccasins? Originally moccasins (an Algonquian word meaning a low-cut shoe created from a single piece of folded leather) were worn by Native American Indians and Eskimos. White colonists who arrived in those lands wearing European shoes ill-suited to the terrain immediately adopted them. Over time, slight differences between one model and another came to signify tribal membership.

Today, things are not that different. The urban prairie teems with moccasins in the modern style, each one indicating a particular way of defining comfort.

One of the most recent styles is the JP, by Tod's, the one with the little balls on the sole, created by Diego Della Valle in 1979, and almost a symbol of the nineties. You could say that this design re-launched the moccasin, transforming it from a fusty object into a fashionable shoe, to the point where it became, in its various guises and seasons, one of the status symbols for the Italian middle classes. In the summer of 2004, Tod's managed to achieve a kind of squaring of the circle by putting heels on their moccasins. Not ordinary, visible heels, which would create a boring governessy look, but a little hidden elevation within the shoe itself. A kind of 'doping' so as not to be a complete flattie, which many women don't care for.

Innovations apart, the traditional 'balled' ones are for ladies on wheels who spend their days accompanying their children from tennis to karate, from German lessons ('*Cara*, we're Europeans now – this is the language of the future') to piano lessons. They're busy mums, who often drive station wagons with automatic gearshifts so as to have one arm free to thump one of their offspring: women who don't need the elevation of heels, as the role of manager of their families has already brought them to the top of their game.

Then there are the rising super-grannies, Milanese fifty-somethings who have always invested in long-lasting shoes for reasons of domestic economy. And nothing, in their eyes, is more long-lasting than a moccasin with a Gucci gold horsebit. They've been wearing them since the seventies; often they own an entire collection, in different colours and finishes. They wear them to lunch with their friends, to play with their grandchildren, and to reproach their daughters, who, for some unknown reason, prefer sports shoes, a reprehensible choice.

These rising super-grannies only abandon their Gucci moccasins during the annual summer exodus to Santa Margherita: in Liguria they prefer wearing sailing shoes, top-siders or Sebagos, worn to accompany their husbands to the harbour. There they stay for an aperitif while the men throw themselves into Paul Cayard for the entire weekend.

In winter time, these ladies repair to Courmayeur, where, to receive their friends, they pull out of the cupboard a slipper-like alternative: Belgian moccasins, inspired by the traditional footwear of Flanders peasants. Made of felt, with leather trimmings and a little tassel in the centre, they ensure that the lady of the house always has a smile on her face. If the lady is left-leaning, and the house in question is not the family apartment in Val d'Aosta but a radical-chic farmhouse in Tuscany, she will be wearing a pair of coloured velvet slippers, known as *friuliane*.

Another fan of comfortable footwear is the Anglophile woman. She has always chosen what are known as penny loafers, or college: the most classic moccasins in the world. When she was young she wore them with a coin in the groove, blushing at the idea that the side you wore the penny indicated whether you were single or already paired up. Later, she got married in a downtown basilica; and when cracks began to appear in the marriage, she consoled herself by moving on from penny loafers to moccasins with high clumpy heels. An utter abomination. And in fact the husband ended up running off with the babysitter.

Trainers: Not Just for Sport

The story of rubber-soled shoes originates from across the seas. Towards the end of the nineteenth century, these were the preserve of the rich, who wore them for elitist sports such as croquet or tennis. The first mass-produced model saw the light of day in America in 1917; The shoes were called – and indeed are still called – Keds. Two years later, Converse All Stars came along, which laced up to the ankle, and were suitable for 'street' sports such as basketball. The same model is still in production.

More than just comfortable, in fact extremely comfortable, this type of footwear, originally designed for sport, is now recommended by all orthopaedic specialists to avoid corns and other deformations of the foot. In appearance at least, the trainer is a non-shoe. Being unisex, it cannot add inches to one's height, and the shape is always more or less the same. What do vary are the colours, brands, and certain extras that distinguish one style from another. Nike, with their 'springs' (Shox Fsm) are radically different from a pair of Adidas designed by the Japanese Yohji Yamamoto, much loved by fashion victims the world over.

There are those of us who buy a new pair each season (with the excellent excuse that, like a used car tyre, a worn sole loses its tread and cannot hold the road) and those who get attached to a particular model that they continue to search for, even after it's no longer produced in their own country.

Among trainer-addicts, for example, there is a kind of sub-group consisting of fans of the Nike Silver, a shoe characterised by a pattern of silver light-reflecting bands, which are also said to be perfect for wearing in winter, being snug, warm and soft. Unfortunately, in the last year they've been chilled down', in other words produced in an even more high-tech and therefore lighter material, which renders them less versatile with regard to changes of season.

Be they 'technical' or 'designer', trainers have become the leisure shoes par excellence, transmitting entirely different messages, depending on by whom and on which occasion they are worn. Thus, whether you like them or not, they too have become a fetish.

The sponsors of this development are sports celebrities (obvious) but also luminaries from the world of music and cinema (less obvious).

Music, in particular hip hop culture, has launched, and continues to launch, ever newer models of trainers (a rapper wearing moccasins or

Church brogues is a rare sight indeed!), immediately taken up by tribes of urban young people the world over.

In reality, show business has appropriated, and, in its turn, taken to the limit a trend that is well established amongst 'ordinary people': an ever increasing attention to physical fitness and, as a consequence, to the steps necessary for obtaining and maintaining it. Here is a statistic that says it all: in the fifties in the US, less than forty million pairs of sports shoes were sold, today it's over three hundred and fifty million.

During this boom, the Nike brand (which was born in 1972, but has gone stratospheric over the last ten years) comfortably dominated the nineties market thanks to avant garde methods of communication, while the eighties were epitomised by Reebok (born in 1982), the shoe of choice for practitioners of Jane Fonda's aerobic workouts, the first trainers specifically designed for a female foot. A flagbearer for this brand was Melanie Griffith in the film *Working Girl*: the story of a New York commuter who arrives at work wearing trainers that she then slips into her bag and replaces with traditional court shoes. The fashion for using two pairs of shoes for the double life of a commuter is in decline, but has not entirely vanished; in March 2004, the American monthly magazine *Lucky* carried out a survey amongst its readers. To the question: 'Do you change your shoes when you get to the office?' 62.4 per cent replied no, while a respectable 37.6 per cent replied in the affirmative. The most telling truth to emerge from this is that women of the new era have a practical sense, and no intention of giving up either comfort or style.

The new millennium opened with a film, *The Royal Tenenbaums*, directed by Wes Anderson, that symbolised a breaking away from Hollywood's cultural norm, as well as offering an entirely new concept of sporting apparel.

At the very moment when Nike was reaching the pinnacle of its success, conquering ever greater chunks of the market, Wes Anderson was bringing to our attention three sportswear brands (not just shoes), which at the time seemed completely out of fashion: Adidas, Fila and Lacoste. Each character in the film was assigned one of these three brands by the director-scriptwriter.

The brainy elder brother (Ben Stiller) was an Adidas aficionado, his neurotic poetess sister (Gwynneth Paltrow) wore only Lacoste, while the jock brother (Luke Wilson) perfectly cloned the look of Björn Borg, uncontested tennis champion of the late seventies and early eighties.

This highly surreal film, supposedly divorced from reality, presaged the crisis in the Nike brand, under fire both from anti-globalisation movements and the fickle caprices of consumers. So much so that today, Nike is increasingly trying to play on its strengths as a high-tech product, for real athletes or wannabes, with the promise of extraordinary sporting performances. It's not a coincidence that one of their latest models plays on the concept of speed: it's called Nike Shox Turbo.

Out of Nike's burgeoning rivals, it's worth mentioning the rebirth of Puma, who, whilst scarcely tweaking the original sixties design, has bounced back into fashion, and was the first to conquer the skateboarding tribes. Puma trainers appear somewhat low-tech, simple in design, more suitable for wearing to a party than attempting to emulate the sporting prowess of the Beckham-Totti-Ronaldo triad. In other words, they do not appear to be part of that ever more pervasive equation: superstar athletes + multinational sponsor = success. And not only this. During the Iraq conflict, pacifist groups over the Internet were inviting people to boycott Nike in favour of the trendy and above all German Puma brand, which originated in a country that refused to support George W. Bush.

Another brand that has attacked Nike 'from the left corner', so to speak, is Adidas. In particular the Gazelle model, which with its evocative low-tech name has become the strolling shoe of choice of the Happy Hour brigade in cities such as Paris and Milan.

Another brand enjoying a fashion moment is Asics, which for many years had been living in the shadows. Testimony (or testimonial, we'll never know) to a burgeoning interest in martial arts,

Quentin Tarantino's latest film *Kill Bill* showcases the actress Uma Thurman with a pair of yellow Asics Trainers, Onitsuka Tigers, on her feet. Originally created for practitioners of t'ai chi, they became an overnight cult classic.

Until the next latest thing comes along, of course.

A Republic Founded Upon Shoes

Winter, 2004. A slanging match on the stage of the Italian Parliament. The Honourable Gabriella Carluccio (centre right) is mocked for her kinky stilettos. All hell breaks loose. Carluccio defends herself with the cry of, 'I refuse to relinquish my femininity for the sake of politics. The Left won't let go of the battles of the past, where in order to prove their worth young girls had to cover themselves up in bulky, mannish clothes. It's we who are the truly liberated women: we wear make-up, high heels, we dress stylishly – we are the new frontier of female emancipation.'

The Honourable Rosy Bindi (centre left), in the habit of wearing low court shoes, rebuts, 'Please! Let's not turn things on their head. They are the ones who want to discriminate, not us, by trying to impose their stereotype of femininity.'

According to the Right, the high heel represents freedom of expression, because it signifies not being afraid of passing for a fool. The high heel is a form of slavery, and liberates only those not wearing it, says the Left. The debate remains ongoing; to tell the truth, it has never been resolved. Italy, a country shaped like a boot, whose national sport is football (played with the foot) has two great passions: politics and sport.

We have the greatest shoe manufacturers in the world, and a bit of argy-bargy between the Right and the Left won't be denied to anyone, from bars to living rooms, right through to the family Christmas lunch.

In other words, tell me what shoes you wear, and I'll tell you who you voted for.

Today, politico-footwear differences are somewhat more subtle (ideologies and walls didn't fall in vain) but during the seventies 'years of lead', a period in Italy of stark extremes, when the Left and Right were locked in bitter, often violent conflict, it was very easy to distinguish 'comrades' from 'fascists'.

Left-leaning boys wore the immortal Clark's desert boots, and indeed recently we have seen them on the feet of the so-called 'giratondini', or anti-Berlusconi protestors; though, given the average age of Nanni Moretti and his cohorts, these are the same young people of yesteryear who simply remained loyal both to footwear and flag.

In the seventies, girls from the Left pounded the streets in (highly uncomfortable) Dutch clogs, and went camping in espadrilles. Their only concession to sex was the high-heeled version of espadrilles, laced around the calf, which, on anything less than perfect legs, made them look like mortadella sausages encased in a net.

Right-wing boys on the other hand favoured Barrow's, a pointy-toed Anglophile shoe that peeked out from the hem of their flares; while the girls couldn't live without their Gucci loafers with gold horsebit, the same shoes that their mothers wore, and never ceased wearing. (See previous chapter.)

In the eighties, during the hedonistic Reagan years, Timberland boots arrived in Italy, which instantly became the footwear of choice for the *paninari*, or sandwich eaters, the new generation of young people who had been so affected by events of the previous decade that they wanted nothing more to do with politics. Timberlands were originally American foresters' shoes, which provided an ideal link between a kind of 'frontier and wide-open spaces' culture and a world of new urban habits and customs. Fast-food restaurants, introduced in Italy during this period, were the big-city headquarters of the *paninari*.

Nowadays, Timberlands fall into the category of leisure shoes, to be worn during cold weather in the fresh air, stripped of all 'tribal' associations.

In the meantime, anti-globalisation movements have demonised fast-food chains for a number of reasons: their exploitation of a low-cost workforce, their standardising of 'tastes' across the world, their heavy dependence on meat in the face of the emerging validation of vegetarian diets, linked to the spread of New Age philosophies.

One of the rallying cries of the anti-globalisation movements is the battle against the big international brands: indeed, one of the most hated is Nike itself, which has been targeted both by Naomi Klein, author of the semi-biblical tract, *No Logo*, as well as the militant documentary maker Michael Moore in his film *The Big One*. Both of these figures are cultural icons for the demonstrators who brought chaos to American campuses at the end of the nineties, organising sit-ins that invited participants to boycott Nike products.

After 11 September 2001, this kind of action quietened down, at least in its more spectacular forms, but it left traces in people's consciences. 'No Global' young people have a fondness for Campers, a Spanish brand of shoes that plays the irony card (some models exist where the left shoe is different from the right). Created from rough-and-ready materials, sometimes even recycled, Campers are the nearest you can get to the ideals of the fashion-conscious nature lover: a marriage of ethics and aesthetics. True purists, however, reject all brands.

Mostly people resign themselves to wearing what they like and what they happen to find. A politically correct shoe has not yet been invented. Whoever manages to come up with one will become the Bill Gates of the century.

The Imelda Syndrome

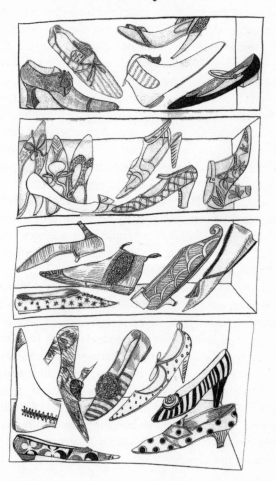

In 1986, fleeing the Philippines to exile in Hawaii, Imelda Romuladez Marcos, wife of the dictator, Ferdinando, was wearing a little pair of dark-blue velvet mules.

Corazon Aquino, who succeeded Marcos to the presidency, put Imelda's shoe collection on public view, 'so·that Filipinos can see how the person who let the people go hungry indulged herself.'

Criticised for her iniquitous taste for luxury, Imelda defended herself by saying; 'It's not true I owned three thousand pairs of shoes. It was only one thousand and sixty.'

Subsequently, Imelda would boast of having come across a sign in a New York shoe shop that read: 'THERE'S A LITTLE IMELDA IN ALL OF US.'

When she returned to Manila from exile in order to stand for the presidency of the republic, she declared, on the eve of the elections, 'Whether I win or lose, tomorrow I'm still going shopping.' She lost.

In 2001, even though her situation had not yet been resolved, Imelda inaugurated a shoe museum in Marikina, the shoe district of Manila. Many of the shoes on display actually belonged to her, having being retrieved from the presidential palace. On this occasion, too, Imelda was ready with a quick-witted one-liner: 'They were looking for skeletons in my cupboard. Instead they only found marvellous objects.'

How can you disagree? In her book, *A Dedicated Follower of Fashion*, Holly Brubach writes: 'A new pair of shoes cannot mend a broken heart, nor cure a headache. But it can certainly alleviate the symptoms.'

Collecting shoes is a phenomenon that exists across all ages and geographical barriers. An Imeldista does not distinguish between height or shape of heels, or colours or finishes, nor does she discriminate between trainers and sandals. An Imeldista does not care if they're a model from a designer's latest collection bought from a boutique or last-year's design from a market stall. An Imeldista hoards. Today, a pair of pink pumps, tomorrow a sporty ankle boot. We're talking about shoes that might only be worn once, because of vagaries of fashion; or bought simply because they were on sale. Shoes that are maybe too big or too tight, but which proved irresistible at the time. When unable to decide between a black pair and a brown pair, the Imeldista usually goes for both.

Her cupboards are groaning, but she's never got the right shoes to wear with that new dress. And so she buys another pair. And maybe yet another, because you never know.

Imeldistas are rarely happy people, at least in terms of their shoe collection. Or rather, they're happy in that magic instant of light-headed folly as they hand over the money. Love at first sight through the illuminated shop window, followed by lightning physical contact in the shop, which they leave with a healthily flushed countenance. The conquest has been made, pleasure causes the blood to throb harder in the veins. And then? And then, just like passion, it's all over. A grubby fingerprint on the upper part of the shoe, a bored glance, regret. 'And I thought they looked so good on me. Adieu.'

The Point of Life

Listening to women, you'd think they all hated a pointed toe. If this were true, it would be impossible to explain the success of certain shoes that are as sharp as knives. In general, pointed shoes make the foot appear longer and slimmer than it really is. Unfortunately, however, it cannot deflect the gaze from other contiguous imperfections: for example, it cannot rescue a footballer's calf nor a less than slender ankle. Indeed, the risk is that it will actually draw attention to these defects, unlike round or square-toed shoes. And yet . . .

The pointed shoe has the attraction of a forbidden game. This is not a coincidence. Its forebear is the *poulaine*, which was in the fifteenth century in common use in France. It was made of cloth, with a pointed toe that could measure anything up to eight centimetres long, and was usually covered in pony skin in order to keep the shape intact. In 1486 it was the subject of a papal bull prohibiting its use, as it was considered to be a symbol of indecent vanity.

Little must have changed, if the fashion of the last five years does not appear to have come up with anything better than pointy-toed shoes. They give the wearer the illusion of occupying a greater territory, and consequently of more power. Teenagers shake off the yoke of childhood the moment they alternate their trainers with a pair of pointy-toed shoes. A woman walking into a men's meeting will use the pointed toe of her shoes to give metaphorical career-orientated kicks to the wearers of classic brogues. She is saying, 'I am here. With these shoes of mine I could actually hurt you. If you don't make me some space, I'll carve some out for myself.'

The anthropologist Desmond Morris compared pointy-toed shoes to one of the cruellest forms of physical maiming: the compression of newborn babies' skulls. This barbarous custom, common among certain primitive cultures of Africa, North and South America and Europe, alters and inhibits the naturally round shape of the head so that one can grow up to be high born. A pointed head is incapable of transporting goods, and therefore must be exclusively occupied with noble affairs of the mind. Up until two centuries ago, a few doctors maintained that the shape of the skull had a bearing on the intelligence of the individual.

In the same way, in China, the feet of aristocratic women were prevented from growing; the harder it was for them to walk, the more noble, revered and waited upon they would be.

Thus, our pointy-toed shoes are merely the symbol of a tribe of particularly intelligent women, whose skills are wasted on manual work, and who are destined for positions of power.

The Unconscious
and The Louis Heel

'I don't know who invented high heels, but all men owe him a lot.'

Thus spoke Marilyn Monroe, the last century's most marvellous wiggler.

But heels don't just come in high or low. They also have different, sometimes highly elaborate shapes. Amongst Yves Saint Laurent's latest offering of sandals, there are some with transparent plexiglass heels, a kind of aquarium, inside which one can see coloured or gilded decorations, as well as sequins in motion, and plenty more besides. There is nothing new in this: already in 1973, there had been perspex heels and platforms.

The artistic variations of the heel actually owe their origins to the court of Versailles. Louis XIV, the Sun King, was of very short stature, which led him to wear heels. Being the kind of man that he was, he wasn't satisfied by a bit of simple elevation: his heels had to depict miniatures of famous battles or idyllic scenes.

In modern times, the king of heels was Roger

Vivier, a French designer who began his career towards the end of the thirties and who, from 1953, collaborated with Christian Dior and other famous couturiers.

His signature pieces were bizarrely shaped and decorated heels, almost a form of jewellery to be worn under the foot. Vivier designed shoes for Marlene Dietrich, Queen Elizabeth (for hre wedding day), Josephine Baker and Catherine Deneuve. Indeed, for the latter, Vivier designed a shoe that was produced by Yves Saint Laurent, and made famous in Luis Buñuel's film, *Belle de Jour:* halfway between a moccasin and a pump, decorated with a square metal buckle.

One of his most famous creations from the early sixties was a heel in the shape of a rose thorn, a kind of magnificent miniature sculpture. Today, the Vivier brand has been brought back to prominence by Diego della Valle, who is relaunching it. The new Viviers are designed by Bruno Frisoni, who has drawn his inspiration from the art of the bygone master, but added a contemporary twist.

For example, a model from his 2004 collection, his first, is called Madame Psy. While the shape recalls the shoe from *Belle de Jour*, the Madame Psy is decorated with myriad little coloured tablets, a kind of ironic tribute to anti-depressive pills. In other words, it's a conceptual shoe inviting neurotic women to abandon their Prozac in favour of a new pair of shoes.

One style Roger Vivier worked extensively with was the Louis heel, which, in its turn, has a long history. Launched at the court of Louis XV, it was then shelved, only to become immensely popular again towards the end of the nineteenth and beginning of the twentieth centuries. Indeed, the boots of the cancan dancers in the Moulin Rouge had Lou's heels. At the eve of the First World War, in the years when the tango craze was at its peak, women danced it in shoes that saw a revival of this coquettish curved heel.

However, whilst the Louis heel has never disappeared from the scene, it hasn't since the turn of the century become the 'must-have' trend of the season.

There are women who love it a great deal. For two reasons: one practical, the other somewhat less so. The first is that the Louis heel is rarely very high; but thanks to its sinuous lines it adds a touch of unmistakable femininity. The second is that the Louis heel is a declaration of personality. It has a retro feel, a reasonable compromise between the narrow fifties 'all woman' heel and the clumpy heels worn by their liberated sisters in the late sixties early seventies, as well as saying a great deal about the wearer: 'I am a creative individual, an independent woman who has a delightful weakness for beautiful objects.'

A Louis woman is someone who, upon entering a shop, invariably replies to the assistant's query of

'How can I help you?' with 'I'm looking for something a little bit different.' The Louis woman has a drawer full of poems, paints watercolours and plays the guitar. Or at least she'd like to do all of these things. Her unconscious is rich and insinuating, she seeks the nuances in human relationships, and can't for the life of her understand how anyone could be so brazen as to ally themselves to current fashion, or, worse still, be utterly, bravely, out of the fashion loop.

Women in Boots

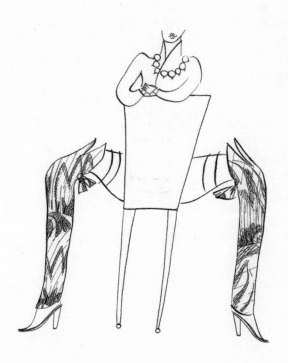

It is said that it was partly thanks to a pair of boots that Joan of Arc ended up burnt at the stake. The Maid of Orleans, apart from poking her nose into thorny theological questions, was in the habit of wearing this kind of footwear, which in those days (and for some time afterwards) was entirely the preserve of men.

Who would hunt, fish, travel and go to war? Men. Therefore men, and men alone, were allowed to wear boots, while women, responsible for domestic chores, wore little cloth slippers, the luxuriousness of which depended on their social status.

Over the centuries, boots have been the de rigueur footwear for pirates and smugglers, while in English 'booty' actually derives from the word 'boot'. It has even lent its name to a record that's been illegally recorded at a concert, a 'bootleg'. A virile symbol of strength and cunning, boots play a starring role in Charles Perrault's classic fairy tale, 'Puss in Boots'.

Until the mid-nineteenth century, the only boots

women were allowed to wear were for riding. Sub-sequently, however, it wasn't just horsewomen and women who did manual labour who were allowed to let their fantasies run wild. In fact, during the belle époque, ankle boots with lots of laces became a kind of everyday equivalent of the corset that was laced around the torso. In Victorian times, short boots were worn to hide the ankle, though ironically, in terms of fashion and morality, they merely exalted it.

However, it was only more recently in the sixties that the female boot was lengthened. Worn with the miniskirt invented by Mary Quant in swinging London, it perfectly epitomised the image of the woman who was freeing herself from all unnecessary frills, as well as sexual and social restraints.

During this period, the idea of a futuristic sex symbol was born out of comic strips and films: Barbarella, played by Jane Fonda in Roger Vadim's 1968 film of the same name, wore a pair of mile-high white boots that had been designed for her by the Italian costumier Giulio Coltellacci.

Away from the silver screen, out on the streets, women were going for the 'space-age' look, as interpreted by Courrèges and Paco Rabanne, the stylists to the stars of that period and their many imitators, while on the radio could be heard the little voice of Nancy Sinatra miaowing, 'These boots are made for walking.'

In the early seventies, two cultural phenomena

found a bizarre common ground. The passion for skiing, in the process of becoming a sport for the masses, combined with an admiration for the feats of astronauts, gave birth to the Moon Boot.

In the following decade, everyone was dancing to 'People from Ibiza.' In Balearic discos, where trends are born which then spread to the rest of Europe, even in August, at the height of summer, people were wearing the soft suede boots inspired by the 'squaw' style.

On the other hand, boots have always been connected to the Wild West. You only have to picture cowboy boots and their ilk: footwear for cowboys, resistant to dust, but fashionable now in the cities. Just like another fashion classic: blue jeans.

Finally, we get to the present day, which offers an infinite number of choices. We have different heel heights and calf fittings; boots come in materials to suit every season and any occasion. After a few years in the wilderness, between the mid-eighties and mid-nineties, boots are back and they're here to stay. There isn't a woman who doesn't own a minimum – and I mean a minimum – of at least two pairs in her wardrobe. You can wear boots with trousers, skirts, with long or short hemlines, by day and by night, at the office and at the weekend.

There are women, perhaps born with sturdy calves, or less than perfect ankles, who begin to love boots once they understand that in this way they can finally get to wear skirts without feeling uncomfortable. There are women who love short skirts, but fear the street-walker effect of completely bare legs. And those who simply feel the cold and have taken to wearing boots because they can no longer bear that icy blade insinuating itself between the hem of one's coat and a pair of shoes that are too light for the winter. There is that (tiny) minority who have been blessed with a fine pair of knees, who know that boots make them appear truly regal. And finally there are those women (and we're back on Imelda territory here) who understand that yes, boots are shoes, but on an entirely different plane and that they are worth collecting even if they do take up rather a lot of space.

Compared to buying a pair of shoes, the purchase of a pair of boots is a far more complex and thus more satisfying affair. Boots stand out and make their presence felt; they greatly influence the overall look of an outfit. Usually, they cost more than a top-brand shoe, and therefore the choice has to be carefully weighed up. In other words, buying a pair of boots is a strategic purchase, just like buying a handbag, which will be used more or less every day.

Those who are not happy with their calves will leave to other women the wearing of those elasti-cated fabric boots with no zip, as they tend to draw attention to the problem rather than hide it. Those with thick ankles would do well to choose boots that are cut generously at the top, thus creating a pleasing tapering optical illusion towards the ankle. Women who prefer decorated or unusually co-loured boots should always pair them up with neutral skirts or outfits, as in this instance the star is – and should be – the boots.

As long as one bears these caveats in mind, long live the boot – the most formidable type of footwear for today's modern world. Personally, I would only advise against their use in the following rare in-stances:

a. Long airline journeys: putting boots back on on arrival is one of the greatest tortures known to woman.
b. Theatrical events by the Italian director Luca Ronconi or films by the Greek, Theo Angelo-poulos: after three hours immobile, feet encased in boots can no longer feel a thing.
c. Clandestine amorous assignations. If you get caught *in flagrante*, precious seconds are lost getting dressed.

Ask Me About the Beatles
(Not those Beatles – the Ankle Boots)

These are basically a less flash, more practical variant of knee-high boots, worn mostly with trousers, though a few brave souls actually dare to wear them with short skirts. This is a risky business, as the leg gets 'cut' at a crucial juncture, and on the whole the look is not kind even to the most proportioned physical types. There is an historical reason for this: the ankle boot was originally intended for men. The first to be associated with them were the Beatles, who subsequently lent their name to the basic model in black leather with elasticated side panels instead of zips known as 'Chelsea Boots' in English and 'Beatles' in Italian. The toe was originally rounded, but eventually became narrower and more pointed as the prevailing musical culture grew more strident, psychedelic and transgressive. Further along down the line, in the punk and grunge years, the original ankle boot morphed into lace-up Doc Martens with their armoured tank of a sole (inspired by military combat boots) and their *noir* urban feel.

Long before spawning the Liverpool Four, Britain had already contributed to the history of the ankle boot, even in a feminine version. The famous Balmorals worn by Queen Victoria, and named after the Scottish royal summer residence, were part fabric, part leather. They remained in fashion as long as women wore skirts that reached the ankle, after which they disappeared from sight.

Much later on, effectively only when the miniskirt arrived on the scene, did the female ankle boot make a comeback, having undergone the same transformation as its 'big brother', the knee-high boot. They adapted themselves to the fashion of the day, appearing in unusual materials (plastic, patent leather, transparent peepholes along the sides), and with square toes and metalwork detail. The most imitated model was Courrèges' Go-go, which was the highest expression of the taste for space-age fashion.

Devotees of ankle boots are a breed apart, a little like those women who are passionate followers of the Louis heel. The ankle boot reveals a kind of core androgyny in its wearer, which, exceptions apart, indicates a woman who is wedded to her trousers. Usually, the collector of ankle boots rather looks down on the 'shoe' shoe, the 'skirt' skirt, and the women who dresses too much like a woman.

The ankle boot hides more of the body than a knee-high, and provides a true carapace for the foot, affirming a decisive personality and one untouched by seductive wiles.

A woman in ankle boots, be they sporty or fancy, is someone who could start a rock band, overturn a board meeting, sell the family firm to set up an *agriturismo*, and other such lunacies. Even more commonly, the woman in ankle boots is already married or engaged, and considers her romantic situation to be bomb-proof.

However, she would be wise not to count her chickens. For most men like the concept of ankle boots about as much as they like pop-socks – in other words, not at all! Though they could be swayed perhaps by a particularly elegant model, maybe one with eccentric detailing and a feminine heel, which leaves absolutely no ambiguous after-taste.

The Pump and the Eternal Illusion of Being Audrey

Pumps are the shoe equivalent of the white shirt: simple and elegant, they are a classic example of chic that doesn't try too hard. Both the white shirt and pumps are inextricably linked to the memory of Audrey Hepburn, a style icon unlike any other.

Audrey was a woman who used her own head. Unlike many of today's starlets who entrust themselves to professional stylists, she would choose her outfits alongside the couturiers who dressed her (Balenciaga and Givenchy, for example) creating styles alongside them. And sometimes without them.

One evening, just before an important event, Audrey accidentally spilt coffee down the outfit she was supposed to be wearing. Picking up any old black skirt, she borrowed one of her husband's white shirts and, tying it around her waist, instantly created a new look.

Similarly, it was she who decided that her height of one metre seventy-five centimetres was quite tall enough, and that, to hell with Hollywood stereotypes, she could permit herself flat shoes without having to compromise one iota of either her sex appeal or femininity.

The creator of the model that today we call the pump was Salvatore Ferragamo, the cobbler born in Irpinia of a large, modest family (he was the eleventh of fourteen children), who in the twenties was to become 'the man who made shoes for Hollywood'. He created footwear for several films, among them *The Ten Commandments* and *The Thief of Baghdad*, and was a friend of Rudolf Valentino, Greta Garbo and Mary Pickford. In the thirties, he returned to Italy and established himself in Florence, where stars and celebrities from all walks of life continued to visit him.

For years, Ferragamo dressed the feet of Queen Elizabeth, the Duke and Duchess of Windsor, the Queen of Italy, Italian actresses such as Sophia Loren and Anna Magnani, and international celebrities such as Carmen Miranda, Marilyn Monroe and Ingrid Bergman. Ferragamo products were – and still are – considered to be the felicitous result of the squaring of the circle: elegant, original shoes that are always extremely comfortable to wear.

Naturally, when Audrey Hepburn arrived in Italy to shoot *Roman Holiday*, she would turn to Salvatore for her shoes, remaining an affectionate client of his until her death.

As a young girl, she had studied dance, and her

ballerina's posture was one element of her natural beauty. It is also why the idea of the pump came to Ferragamo. The patent for this shoe was only deposited at the State Central Archives in 1957, but the product had been manufactured at least three years previously. In the original drawing, preserved at the Ferragamo Museum, you can see perfectly well how the designer transformed a real ballet pump into an everyday walking shoe.

Still using Audrey as his muse, Ferragamo created another version of the pump: a low-cut shoe with a very low and graceful heel, which, from then on, has been called the Sabrina heel, after the unforgettable film of the same name in which the actress starred.

Now, as we haven't all been born as tall and genetically chic as Audrey Hepburn, choosing the ballerina shoe, depending on your viewpoint, can either be seen as an act of extreme courage or extreme arrogance.

There are two categories of pump-wearers. The first consists of little queens of understatement, impervious to the clamorous demands of fashion. These particularly beautiful and well-proportioned creatures don pumps with nonchalance; and, knowing they have no need to, do not wear make-up, and only the same few pieces of jewellery. To these perfect, Audrey-like creatures, one can offer no reproach.

The second category sees pumps as aspirational

objects; and by wearing them, these poor deluded creatures think they will become as chic as Audrey. Sorry to disappoint them but it's just not that easy. If there is one shoe in the world that demands fine ankles, and above all a perfect foot and impeccable bearing, it is in fact the pump. In most models, the arch of the foot is neither lifted nor supported, and there is the risk of slopping around as though one were in slippers. In other words, pumps are very lovely, but not terribly helpful. And yet, it is unusual to find a woman who doesn't own at least one pair. In fact, many would call them their favourite shoes, the ones they wear day in, day out, and which, once they get worn out, are replaced by an almost identical pair.

Some men like pumps. These are mostly short blokes, who don't like being overshadowed by an overly imposing companion. The story of Tom Cruise, ex-husband of the beanpole Nicole Kidman, is a universal one. Upon their divorce, Nicole let the newspapers know that she now had at least one reason to be happy: she could finally wear heels.

However, most men just don't like pumps. They sulk when we want to watch *Breakfast at Tiffany's* for the hundredth time to rejoice in Audrey's elegance. They tell us that women like Audrey as a style icon, but that she wasn't the least bit sexy. These are men who think that sexiness is all down to the height of your heels. Men who never clocked the appearance of Brigitte Bardot on this planet. Another great pump-wearer, but one who interpreted them in her own way, and in doing so became the walking symbol of a wild, free sensuality.

The other Hepburn and Men's Shoes

Katharine Hepburn was the product of a suffragette mother and a doctor father. As a young girl, she was reared in the cult of modernity and independence. Thus, even though she chose to enter the superfical Hollywood world of bright lights and illusion, Katharine interpreted the role of diva, and the star system, in her own unique way. She loathed skirts, above all because they obliged her to wear suspenders, and therefore almost always wore trousers. Who knows, if she had been born in the era of tights, she might never have created the extraordinary, much copied, androgynous style that made her famous. Her wide trousers perfectly complemented the men's shoes that she would have made to measure.

The first famous woman to choose men's shoes and make them fashionable in the twenties was Eleanor Roosevelt, the little sister of the American President, Theodore. Wife of another president, Franklin Delano, who was also a distant cousin, Eleanor often wore a kind of primitive lace-up shoe known as the Oxford, which was not just a fashion choice. The First Lady did a great deal for the female cause: she offered herself up as a strong-minded leader, representing an entire generation of women, who, having grown up between two World Wars and the Depression, were out of touch with useless frivolities. Already, during the First World War, female fashion had changed: skirts were shorter and looser, made from more robust, cheaper materials. But the most important change was the disappearence of the corset, an atrocious instrument of torture reserved for our sex. One of the slogans of the day, printed on American government leaflets, was 'LOOSE HIPS BUILD SHIPS'. The wives, mothers and girlfriends of men at war could not have worn anything but low, comfortable shoes, suitable for riding a bicycle, going out to work, procuring rationed food, and, in Europe, running away from bombs. In those days, women were merely soldiers in civvies.

Pretty soon, beneath the glamorous lights of cinema, androgynous shoes were to acquire different, less severe nuances. Worn by stars such as the eccentric, mysterious and gay Greta Garbo, lace-up shoes acquired a touch of ambiguity. On the feet of another diva, Marlene Dietrich, they even launched a new look of elegance and sex appeal. The German actress and singer was an expert lover of shoes, who was wont to say, 'Shoes are much more important than frocks or suits. They provide elegance to an entire look. My advice is to buy one pair of excellent-quality shoes, as opposed to three cheap pairs, or ones that you're not entirely sure of.'

Of the two hundred pairs of shoes owned by Dietrich, there were many lace-up, two-toned models, known in the trade as Spectators. They were originally created as walking shoes for wealthy men, to be worn exclusively in warm weather, often made of cream-coloured fabric, with only the point, the heel and the middle of the upper in leather.

Marlene adopted them at once, wearing them beneath her beloved trouser suits. Around the same period, Coco Chanel was inspired by the same two-tone motif to create her own cult shoe, a classic that has not dated: a cream-coloured upper, with a black rounded toe in either leather or patent.

Mademoiselle Chanel admitted to having designed those shoes in order to make her own feet, which she found too large, appear smaller. She was right; the optical illusion never fails.

While we're on the subject of optical illusions, remember, if you wear light-coloured shoes, never wear dark tights, and vice versa. This lesson comes once again courtesy of Marlene Dietrich. Whether in a skirt or trousers, the Blue Angel never wore stockings that contrasted with her shoes. The chromatic uniformity of shoe and stocking had the instant effect of lengthening the leg. We, girls of the new millennium, should take heed of Marlene's words, because, let's face it, she was someone who knew a thing or two about legs.

A Brief Course in Self-esteem
(About the Length of a Shoestrap)

In footwear terms, a shoe with a strap is what Vladimir Nabokov's *Lolita* is to the male fantasy: ingenuous in appearance, perverse in substance. The basic design of this type of shoe (comprising a round or square toe, and a fairly low strap in relation to the arch) is known in the trade as Mary Jane. The name derives from a kind of children's slipper worn by Mary Jane, the little sister of the early twentieth-century comic-strip character, Buster Brown. In this case too, their most famous ambassador was an actress, a baby diva by the name of Shirley Temple.

Since then, the Mary Jane has gone through a tremendous evolution. There are versions that call to mind the real children's shoes, while others have a medium-height heel, often a Louis, recalling the dance shoes of the twenties. Finally, there are models where the base has been widened and the toe enlarged into a kind of gigantic biscuit, such as Campers. Very recently, the stylist Marc Jacobs referred to Mary Janes in order to exalt childhood in cartoon form. But this is not the point; the point is that Mary Janes are, par excellence, the shoe with a strap. Straps, which can be found on very high sandals, on stiletto court shoes, on reinterpreted pumps, are a lethal detail. They can destroy even the most beautiful legs, the finest ankles. They exalt skinniness, and create the illusion of chubbiness. They can even make the skirt above them appear ugly. I say skirt, because wearing strappy shoes with trousers is what some people do, but nevertheless it remains a cowardly, turncoat act.

Thus, to wear this kind of shoe, you need to have a highly developed sense of self-esteem. They're for very confident women, who believe utterly in their own existence, regardless of the shoes they're wearing. In other words, an endangered species indeed – the heroic pandas of femininity.

Oh, and another small detail, there's the problem of fastening the bloody strap. The buckle always comes loose, the little hole you stick the pin in is never where you want it to be, and you often end up having to fasten it any old way, only to discover that in the briefest interval of time it has become too big. Not only that, but classic Mary Janes don't even have buckles on the end of the straps, but buttons, often coated in slippery varnish – a diabolical invention that breaks nails and invites malediction. This is why a pair of Mary Janes, in spite of never having been worn much for all of the above-mentioned reasons, ends up being put out to pasture earlier than other shoes, because the strap has broken, and the shoe-repairer implacably decrees that there's nothing to be done. Thus the Mary Jane is the most insidious of shoes, just as Lolita is the most insidious of women.

The Law of the Heel

Instinctively I feel like saying: girls, boycott mules! They're tricky, unreliable shoes. For a start, it's hard to buy them in the right size. In the shop, your foot slides this way and that way, and it's never quite clear if they're a comfortable fit. Well, take it from me, mules are not comfortable shoes.

Mules are not made for walking in. They are shoes born of centuries of indoor living in the houses of the rich and the powerful, reaching their highest expression in the mid-seventeenth century. Even then, the mule was more of a frivolous accessory than a real shoe; an *objet* of skilled craftsmanship, created to showcase embroidery, precious fabrics such as velvet and brocade, gems, and other decorative gewgaws. Mules were the caprice of kings, queens and courtesans, who stayed inside the palace or travelled around in a carriage.

Mules were born flat, then raised up on heels, but it was above all in the uppers, that the master slipper-makers really let their imaginations run riot.

Basically, the little slipper that evolved into what today we call a mule is a bit like a tapestry. Now tell me: today, what would you do with a tapestry? Nothing.

And we with our tapestry mules are supposed to get around, maybe even in cities such as Rome or Florence, where irregular cobblestones are just waiting to send us flying.

It must also be said that any shoes that leave the heel exposed are never comfortable. And the heel can be bare in a number of situations: perched atop a mule, a classy sandal, or even inside a pair of Dutch clogs. It seems impossible that there were women who willingly chose to suffer in clogs: the victims of ankle sprains during the feminist rallies of the seventies remain too numerous to be counted.

In mules, the heel searches in vain for its permanent centre of gravity. Let's get things straight: the heel is not a beautiful thing to behold. All men think this, though few admit it; for them, the sexy part of the foot is the toes. To think that in Victorian times the heel was considered to be obscene, the foot equivalent of the female bottom. Bonkers. Today, a heel is only a little on the ugly side, too dry and white if not looked after properly. Before such a sight, the male libido plummets, just as when faced with a pair of teddy-bear-patterned pyjamas.

The only instance, apart from on the beach, in which the sight of a heel is acceptable, is the Chanel shoe: closed at the toe, open at the back, but with a strap around the heel.

Here too, the ingenious Coco had a revolutionary insight. Women like the idea of mules, she thought, but as flapping shoes are not an attractive look she found a way of securing the wandering foot with a strap that supports the back of the ankle, conferring stability and decency in one stroke.

Unfortunately, as is the case with many of Chanel's inventions, this style of shoe has achieved such classic status that it has become almost boring. And yet there are situations where it is worth considering, for example, going to the office in the summer, or a spring wedding. Or when a *décolleté* is too much, and a sandal too little, a Chanel shoe, perhaps in a slightly unusual colour, is simply perfect.

Take to Your Platforms!

In the third act of *Hamlet*, the Prince of Denmark lays into poor Ophelia for being too vain, thundering: 'I have heard of your paintings too, well enough; God hath given you one face, and you make yourselves another: you jig, you amble . . . and make your wantonness your ignorance.'

According to Shakespeare scholars and British fashion historians, 'you jig, you amble' is a reference to none other than *chopines*, the towering stacked shoes that were the fashion of the day. More than shoes, these were veritable pedestals that could reach as high as fifty centimetres, which ladies would be lifted up on to by the sturdy arms of their maidservants. The fashion for *chopines* orginated in Venice, first amongst prostitutes, then amongst respectable ladies. According to some sources, they came over from Turkey, where these stilt-like shoes were used in the hammam to keep the feet raised above ground and dry. Others say they originated in Spain, where there was an abundance of cork, a light material·ideally suited to stilts.

Whatever its origins, this Venetian fashion spread all over Europe, and Elizabeth I of England was one of its followers. Hamlet's outburst was thus also taking a pop at the Sovereign, who owned a collection of *chopines*.

The *chopines* craze was as brief as it was excessive; already, by the early 1600s, women had climbed down from their stilts. And there, on the ground, they would remain.

Until, just before the Second World War, in Florence, Salvatore Ferragamo showed the prototype of his first 'platforms' to one of his clients, the Duchess Visconti di Modrone. Appalled, the noblewoman declared, 'Salvatore, these shoes are an abomination! What *were* you thinking of?' To which Ferragamo replied, 'Duchess, I ask you a small favour. Wear these shoes tomorrow to Sunday Mass; if even one of your friends compliments you on them, I'll make you a pair of shoes for free to your own design.'

That Sunday in church the ladies of Florence only had eyes and words for the Duchess's shoes. And thus, platforms were to rule throughout the forties. They turned out to be practical and economical, innovative in their shape and design. Ferragamo, and other designers after him, created diverse decorative patterns, and thus the 'stilts' principle shifted over to sandals, closed shoes, day footwear and evening footwear.

However, after the war, the curtain fell on the

platform shoe; it was too reminiscent of the years of economic isolation and misery. For women, too, it was love at first sight with the stiletto heels that were such an ideal accompaniment to the new look proposed by Christian Dior.

Platforms would make their comeback in the early seventies, under the bright new lights of glam rock. Bisexuality, eccentricity, excess and sequins were the look that accompanied the music of the day. Elton John, David Bowie, and T. Rex's Marc Bolan were photographed wearing brightly coloured boots and shoes with impossibly high platforms – sometimes reaching eighteen centimetres. Street fashion followed suit: the dominant look consisted of fitted jackets and tight – very tight – trousers that clung to the sexual organs and flowed out like bell bottoms over gigantic platform shoes.

It was an era of 'glittering' fashion, so over-the-top as to appear decadent – the guttering of the revolutionary flame that had blazed a decade earlier in swinging London. Already, by 1977, the dancer John Travolta (Tony Manero in *Saturday Night Fever*) had lowered his platforms by several centimetres. From then on, the male platform shoe virtually disappeared, only making an appearance as an oddity in transsexual shows, as a kind of parody of femininity.

However, for women, the platform shoe continues to wax and wane according to the vagaries of fashion. The Spice Girls brought it back in for a couple of seasons; and every now and then it reappears, but by and large it remains an embarrassment (perhaps thanks to its saucy origins among the prostitutes of Venice) that you either love or hate.

Platforms are popular with women who want to appear taller but can't abide traditional narrow high heels. Eccentrics also like them because, if well designed, the shoe is transformed into a kind of sculptured pedestal.

Yet at the same time there exists an entirely different category of women who will not even hear them mentioned. Platforms, be they low or high, are perceived as being vulgar, showy and crass. When we denigrate platforms, we are unwittingly slipping into Hamlet-mode – a poetic moralist who was also a royal pain, and unqualified in matters of fashion.

In truth, the platform shoe, particularly the pure forties style, can be extremely elegant, providing it is worn with an appropriate outfit. For example, while it looks wonderful with a flowery silk frock that flows down to the knee, it is an abomination matched up with a tight-fitting pencil skirt. Platforms with miniskirts are strictly forbidden; as are platforms with drainpipes, or worse still, pedal pushers.

On the other hand, if you wear platform sandals under a pair of trousers in an elegant fabric, worn long enough to skim the upper of the shoe, you'll walk like a queen. I happened to meet Monica Bellucci dressed like this, and never did a pair of platforms appear so elegant.

Globalisation and the Crisis
in the Western Slipper

While we're all capable of looking elegant in a pair of evening sandals or shoes, it's trickier trying to maintain a certain dignity in slippers. Just the name itself is a downer. And to think that in distant times the slipper was an object of luxury, indeed a status symbol: as a mark of respect, one would kiss those of popes, bishops and cardinals! Nowadays a slipper-wearer is a sullen, enervated creature, lacking in vitality and interests, apart from his remote control for channel hopping, which he can do quite easily regardless of whichever abominations he's wearing on his feet.

This is why, in noughties households, slippers are either exhibits from a horror museum or in the best-case scenario exotic souvenirs.

If you want to learn more about your increasingly mysterious neighbours, go and knock on their door around suppertime with an innocuous request for an onion or a pinch of salt. This way you'll catch them unawares, and by seeing what they wear on their feet, in those moments when a sense of decorum flags, you'll find out whom you really share the roof of your apartment building with, and the arial on top of it.

There are fathers of Daddy's girls, who, in order to make their little darlings happy, walk around the house with two gigantic furry Disney ducks on their feet; and mothers of spoilt, Playstation-addicted sons, who please themselves by wearing Chip the squirrel on one foot, and Dale on the other. There are fifty-year-old women who in public boast of their travels, but who only during a bit of late-night TV-viewing in the presence of Gigi Marzullo dare to wear a certain pair of extremely pointed Moroccan slippers with a lingering smell of goat. Then there's a flock of chilly ladies and young women who, even in Naples, either opt for coloured *friuliane* velvet slippers (until recently, only to be found in Venice); or else skid around the floor in thick boiled-wool socks embroidered with edelweiss that they bought at Cortina d'Ampezzo.

At supper, in the most unlikely Italian households, will appear slippers fit for a Turkish Grand Vizier ('I got them at the market in Istanbul for a song'), little Chinese slippers as modelled by the Gang of Four (in these cases, usually the entire family democratically opts to wear them), even splendid, crimson-velvet Burmese thongs, so beautiful that it's almost a waste to wear them indoors, considering what a statement they'd make out on the street.

Thus, the modern slipper is as robustly multiethnic as the world we live in. Nothing wrong with that – we're globally content about this state of affairs. But certain crucial questions remain, which hopefully in the future will be answered.

Firstly, what became of the dignified, slightly sad-looking smooth leather slippers our parents and grandparents used to wear? I would imagine that the bulk of them are now destined for places like Turkey, China or Burma, while we amuse ourselves with these nations' offerings, but I can't be certain of this conjecture.

A second question: what happened to *pattine?* These were little cloth squares to be worn beneath shoes, which were at the height of their popularity in the early sixties, coinciding with a boom in electric floor-polishers. All mothers insisted they should be worn, and 'I don't want marks on my floor' was the shriek that would greet one upon entering the house. Today, adieu *pattine*, adieu mother's housewifely little foibles, and adieu to those floors that resembled the skating rink in *Holiday on Ice*.

A third and final question: what happened to those ladies' slippers with a little heel and a tuft of pink marabou feathers on the front, which Marilyn Monroe wore in *The Seven Year Itch*? I saw one of the last-remaining pairs, kitsch and sublime, in Moda Stile, a dusty, old-fashioned shop in Verona. I considered buying a pair as a souvenir from a bygone era. I'm sorry now that I didn't, as the shop is no longer there: it's become a jeans outlet.

Rain: a Divine Punishment

In the winter of 1985, there was an immense snow-fall in Northern Italy that lasted several days. News reports testified to an interesting escalation in the use of protective footwear against what one journal-ist called 'the white visitor.' Day one: optimism, normal shoes. Day two: heavier shoes, with rein-forced rubber soles. Day three: fur-lined boots. Day four onwards: moon boots for après ski were the order of the day, and indeed some people were spotted wearing hi-top fishing boots on the under-ground, the only transport system left running in Milan during that period.

This episode illustrates how remaining elegant in the snow or rain is a virtual impossibility. Further-more, it might even be said that inclement weather rains down from the sky in order to castigate female vanity.

This is extremely well demonstrated in a fairy tale by Hans Christian Andersen, 'The Girl Who Trod on the Loaf.' The author of 'The Red Shoes,' another tale in which shoes bring nothing good, outdoes himself this time in terms of dark moralism.

Inge, the heroine of 'The Girl Who Trod on the Loaf,' is a pretty and flirtatious little maid, who owns a pair of delectable new shoes. Inge's kind mistress persuades her to take some bread to her poor old mother whom she has left behind in her village. Inge, wickedly, has no intention of going to visit her mother, of whom she is ashamed. The only reason she agrees to her mistress's request is that it will provide a good opportunity for preening in front of the villagers. On the way, in order not to dirty her shoes in the mud, she uses the loaves of bread to wade through the marshes; her punishment for this is to fall in. Her feet remain stuck to her shoes, a fate that also befalls the unlucky heroine of 'The Red Shoes,' while the loaves are embedded into the heels, thus condemning Inge to starve unto eternity.

It must have been in order to avoid a similar end that vain New Yorkers, during the particularly harsh winter of 2003–2004 (18 degrees below zero) took to wearing the Australian boots called Uggs. They became an instant cult, once they were photographed on the feet of women like Kate Moss, Madonna and Demi Moore. Apparently, word has it that they are so warm you can wear them without socks, even in a snow storm.

That's as may be, but the truth is that we women are usually put on the spot even by a common or garden downpour. I have a friend, an extremely elegant antiquarian, who admits she can't bring herself to buy any kind of 'walking shoe', especially the kind designed for unknown terrain and bad weather.

It matters little if Burberry has come up with wellington boots in their trademark tartan, or that you can also buy Chanel wellingtons. At the end of the day, they're still wellies: i.e., shapeless rubber objects suited to guerrillas, or members of the Home Guard, in bad weather.

It's no coincidence that the term 'galoshes' derives from the Gauls; once the Romans had conquered them, they stole from them the idea of covering their boots with leather strips to protect against the rain.

These primitive galoshes were in essence a kind of overshoe, similar to those worn in the nineteenth century. Andersen also devoted a story to this kind of footwear, but unlike 'The Red Shoes' and 'The Girl Who Trod on the Loaf', it deals with their positive, magical virtues. The overshoes, gift of a fairy, have the power instantly to transport the wearer to any place and epoch of their choice – space and time being no obstacle.

Who knows, maybe they're due for a comeback.

What Men Say
When They Talk about Shoes

It is well-known that when women fall in love they commit several errors. One of these is not paying attention to men's shoes. We're so wrapped up in what's on our own feet that we scarcely give a second glance to theirs. For example, is it possible to fall in love with a man wearing diarrhoea-coloured woven-leather moccasins? No, it's not, and yet, let me assure you, it happens. Not just because love is blind, but because we women are so ignorant about men's shoes.

Usually, when a woman accidentally strays into the men's department of a shoe shop, she yawns, then beats a hasty retreat. Bad, very bad. Girls, in search of either a husband, or just companionship, would do well to become expert in the field, because a sizeable number of men might find this irresistibly appealing.

Men are mostly pretty well informed about what's on their feet, without necessarily going to the lengths of the actor Daniel Day Lewis, who, during a sabbatical year from acting, apprenticed himself to a Florentine shoemaker.

So what do men make of a woman who can help them choose a pair of shoes? Pretty much the same as what they think of a woman who understands the offside rule: i.e., that she's the tops. Naturally, being men, they don't want a woman to be better informed than they are, as that would be dangerous. Still, it's worth knowing the basic differences between types of shoes; whatever happens, it's a great opening gambit, and in the best-case scenario, you might actually find yourself helping him choose shoes for his, and indeed *your*, wedding.

Should you be successful, it is worth bearing in mind a few fundamental differences between male and female shoe-lovers. Men brush and polish their shoes with loving care, while it is a well-known fact that we find this chore to be insufferably boring. Men appreciate shoes that last, while women prefer to keep changing theirs. Finally, unlike women who choose on a whim, men always have a clear idea as to which shoes suit what: i.e., lace-ups for the office, black for special occasions, loafers for leisure time, heavy ankle boots for inclement weather, docksiders for sailing, and so forth – all highly practical, and, from where we're standing, utterly devoid of all imagination. Which is how it should be, guys – leave the over-the-top stuff to us!

However, cohabitation between shoe-lovers of different sexes is possible. In order to get the ball rolling, it is helpful for women to be au fait with the basic rules of the world of men's shoes. Dear reader, stay with me at this point, and try not to yawn. There follow five opening gambits to leave your male interlocutor open-mouthed with astonishment:

1. Men's shoes began to differentiate themselves from women's towards the end of the fifteenth century, rumoured to be all thanks to a physical defect of Charles VIII of France. The King, who reigned from 1493–1498, had six toes on his feet, and as a result would have particularly wide-toed square shoes made for him. This fashion spread across Europe, and reached England, where Henry VIII and his court began wearing shoes whose soles were seventeen centimetres wide. The wider the sole, the richer and more powerful you were seen to be.

2. The eighteenth century saw the fashion for gigantic buckles, the nineteenth favoured romantic decoration, but the turning point for the modern male shoe came towards the end of the nineteenth century. Europe began to import American models, which, with continual modifications, bring us to the present day. The main ones are Bostons or Oxfords (lace-ups); Bulldogs (a half-boot with a buttoned flap in the front); Derbys (two-tone Oxfords). Even loafer moccasins come from the United States, originally part of the 'preppie' look, as worn by nice boys from expensive preparatory schools.

3. High boots, worn throughout the ages, saw their popularity plummet after the Second World War. They were considered to be inextricably linked with the image of Nazism and Fascism, though who knows, maybe at some point their moment will return.
4. The pointed male shoe, fashionable in Edwardian times, made a neo-dandy comeback with the advent of Teddy Boys.
5. Desert boots, leisure footwear of the fifties, are merely a more sophisticated version of the boots worn by General Montgomery's Eighth Army in Egypt.

The Mysterious Magic of Red Shoes

There is an Anglo-Saxon proverb that goes: 'Red and Yellow/To catch a fellow.' Nowadays, unless you've set your sights on a Roma or Lecce fan (red and yellow being the colours of both clubs), I doubt whether pairing up these two garish colours would lead to any particularly interesting results.

That said, red shoes – and only red shoes – merit a chapter of their own. In fact, a little poem. (Oh, all right then, a rhyme.) Here it is:

On display, in the window of a shop
A red shoe, you'll find, is always top.
Low-heeled, or high-heeled, with a buckle,
   or without
The red shoe's the one that always stands out.

The others are all brown, or maroon, or black,
Fun is what those colours lack.
While a red shoe is wild and full of high jinx
Turning a woman into a playful minx.

A red shoe brings endless good fortune
That can even reach the moon,
A red shoe is a charm,
That will keep you from harm.

'They're *so* last season, I'm chucking mine,'
Say the know-all girls – we know their kind.
But don't listen to them, just follow your heart,
Give your feet wings – from your red shoes
  don't part.

And when your aunt says they're not respectable,
That in such a colour, you'll be a spectacle,
You calmly reply, 'I couldn't give a damn,
'I intend to own as many as I can.'

Wearing red shoes will give your day wings,
Energy, pizzazz, and other such things!
Put them on, and a witch you'll become,
Sexy and powerful, all rolled into one.

Trade Secrets and Other Devilment

The most popular heel height in production is between five and seven centimetres, known in shoemaking jargon as between fifty and seventy points.

The highest heel you can get is nine centimetres, though on rare occasions this can be ten centimetres.

Shoes used on the catwalk can go up to twelve centimetres, but they are almost always lowered to ten centimetres before reaching the high street.

A heel under five centimetres can have several variations: a pump can range from nought to one and a half centimetres, while a moccasin is around three centimetres.

Short women tend to go for high heels, while those taller than one metre seventy centimetres often suffer from the same syndrome that befell the beanpole Nicole Kidman when she was married to the vertically challenged Tom Cruise – i.e., trying not to tower over him.

In truth, there are no hard and fast rules. Just lots of women of different heights and with different viewpoints. There are short and tall women who would quite happily climb mountains in nine-centimetre heels, and actually feel uncomfortable wearing trainers, which half the world consider to be the *non plus ultra* of comfort.

On the other hand, certain women don't like heels, but still wear them, either because it's the done thing, or else because they think they look better in them. You can recognise these women as they totter along looking worried and in pain. They've got the look of those kids who are used to dressing in jeans and sweatshirts, then suddenly have to wear a suit and tie to present their university thesis.

It's impossible to be either attractive or elegant if you go around looking awkward. Thus everyone needs to find the heel that suits them, as every height commands its own posture; what one person finds comfortable might not be so for another.

To avoid rash purchases, next time take a ruler and measure the heel height of the shoes you wear most often. There's nothing wrong with wearing the same kind of heel; in fact you avoid having to take up and let down your trousers *ad libitum*, while once and for all you establish your manner of walking, or, in a nutshell, your style.

Not only that, but a consistent deportment will prevent that annoying question that always makes us feel like frauds: 'How come you look so tall today? Are you wearing heels?'

Health and Shoes:
a Topic that Won't Be Broached

Even Naomi Campbell, a creature with the bearing of a panther, once stumbled and fell on a catwalk because of a pair of shoes that were too high. You need to know how to walk on certain shoes, and by doing so too often you can risk more than the occasional tumble.

Some experts in podiatry maintain that a 'MAY DAMAGE YOUR HEALTH' sign should appear on heels over nine centimetres high, as is already the case on cigarette packets.

An exaggeration? Not really. Artificially compressing the extremities causes harm. Chinese women whose feet were bound to stop them growing suffered severe skeletal problems, from osteoporosis to arthritis, as did elderly Western women who spent the fifties tottering around on stilettos, which were the fashion of the day.

What fate, therefore, lies in store for the bones of this generation who are slaves to even more killer heels? Osteopaths claim it is still too early to tell, but admit that the construction of today's shoes (softer materials, more care devoted to the anatomical shape of the inner sole) would appear less harmful.

In the meantime, however, in order to be able to wear certain kinds of terribly narrow pointed shoes, many women will do anything, including going under the surgeon's knife.

In New York, in her luxurious Park Avenue clinic, the podiatrist Suzanne Levine operates on six pairs of feet a week, at fifty thousand dollars a pop. The most popular operation is the 'filing', or in severer cases the elimination, of bunions. Even the Italian TV presenter Paola Barale has admitted to undergoing a similar operation, claiming, 'I didn't use to like my toes, but now I can wear any sandals I like.'

As for other mini-operations in demand to look better in shoes, these range from ankle and calf liposuction to subcutaneous injections of silicone gel to soften up areas in the foot that rub against shoes that are either too high or too tight. These are the ridiculous excesses of the times, where we can't stomach the slightest physical imperfection, or do without the latest fashion. Without being too alarmist, it is still possible to pick up some useful advice from this state of affairs:

Ten Rules for Happy Feet

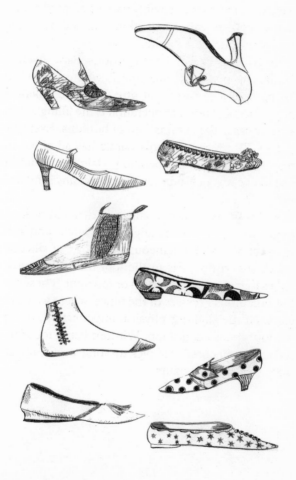

1. Know that as you get older feet tend to get longer and wider. It's useless trying to squeeze into your usual size 37; probably after the age of forty you'll be a 38.
2. Remember that, whatever your age, Audrey Hepburn advised buying shoes half a size bigger than necessary, as comfort is integral to elegance.
3. For the same reason, it is a good idea to buy shoes in the evening, when feet are at their biggest, and never in the morning.
4. Whether you're buying heels or flatties, never get shoes that aren't instantly comfortable: the 'breaking in' myth needs debunking.
5. Try not to wear the same pair of shoes for too many days in a row. In fact, ideally you should change them every day, so as to avoid their losing their shape, and the feet getting used to a single contour.
6. Whenever you get the chance – at home or on the beach – try and walk around barefoot.

7. After an evening of walking on heels, massage the soles of your feet with a tennis ball.
8. Look at the feet of your mother and grandmother. Many small deformations are hereditary, and therefore preventable.
9. If your feet ache, or are often reddened on the sides, find a good specialist and visit them as often as you would the dentist.
10. Whatever kind of shoes you wear and whatever the shape of your feet, accept and love them, pampering them with love and pedicures. They are a pedestal for your beautiful soul.

Perfect Maintenance

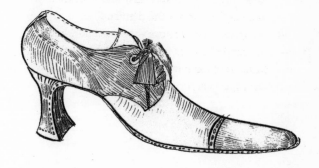

'A good clean will lengthen the life of your shoe, which is now a question of national importance. Your shoes will last longer if you paid a decent amount for them, and if you keep them well-polished and soled, and in a state of good repair.' These pearls of wisdom appeared in the June 1941 edition of English *Vogue*: the War was on, money was tight, and a great respect abounded for the nation's most popular means of transport.

Nowadays, caring for your shoes is not only a good way of saving money, but is also a way of showing love towards these uniquely special objects. Besides which, a woman can be dressed to the nines, but dusty shoes or worn-out heels are as bad as chipped nail polish or, worse still, laddered tights. So, grab your tube of polish, and let's have some elbow grease.

1. Only use suitable products; never get tempted to make your own concoctions.
2. Leather is a delicate, living material.

3. Always brush your shoes before wearing them. Consider this as necessary as combing your hair before going out.
4. To stop shoes getting ruined in the rain, protect them with a water-repellent spray: this also works well on suede. Once you get home after a downpour, let your shoes dry out in shoe forms, then give them another spray. These days, you can buy excellent, reasonably priced plastic shoe forms that are more practical than the wooden ones reserved for true shoe-lovers. And what about the old trick of stuffing them with newspaper? They'll dry quickly, but the shoes won't reacquire their original shape.
5. If a pair of shoes wears out after you've only worn them a few times, don't accept it: take them back to the shop, demanding a repair or substitute. This is your right, especially if you paid a lot for them.
6. If a pair of boots you have bought turns out to be unexpectedly tight on the calves, don't give them away to a skinnier friend. Ask the shop-keeper to stretch the leg.
7. As far as trainers go, there are people who put them in the washing machine, but the experts advise washing them with a soft brush and a mixture of water and liquid soap or mild detergent. Marks on the leather trimming can be removed with cotton wool dipped in milk, or in extreme cases Tippex.

How a shoe is designed and produced

There is certainly an artistic element in creating a shoe. Pierre Hardy, a designer for Dior when the *maison* was under Gianfranco Ferre, and since 1990 a creator for Hermès, actually studied the plastic arts. Famous for his perfectly proportioned heels, he claims they are 'able to define the silhouette of a woman, just like the final brushstroke in a painting.'

Becoming an accessories designer is not easy. Sara Porro, the thirty-seven-year-old creative force behind Tod's bags and shoes, also has her own line, Dove nuotono gli squali, or Where Sharks Swim. She studied at Milan's Istituto Marangoni, and like everyone else, thought she would become a clothes designer. By chance, her first job was assistant to an accessories designer, and thus her career was born. Sara considers herself to be very lucky: she entered this world at the right time, just when accessories were becoming an important part of fashion. Today, those working in her field for the big names are few and highly sought after. But how do you design a shoe?

'Inspiration can come from any source,' says Sara. 'You have fashion, which means a collection of clothes, that can suggest a trend. Then there is personal research. You study vintage shoes from flea markets, but also seemingly incongruous objects. In a dog's boutique in New York, I bought some very pretty collars: I just had the feeling they'd stimulate new ideas. A few seasons back, I designed a collection inspired by Lapland; as well as adding a twist to their traditional decorations, I was inspired by the colours and images of the sky there. While this is the cultural aspect of my work, there is also a practical side that consists of field research. I listen very carefully to the women around me, to their enthusiasm for, or complaints, about any particular model. When I have a picture in my head, when I have chosen the leit motif of the new collection, I start designing the "hero piece" of a series.'

Once the design has been approved, a last is created from a piece of wood, which will then be covered by leather or pre-selected materials.

The standard size of this last, equivalent until recently in clothes terms to an Italian 42, or UK 10, was a shoe-size 36, a UK 3. But as the size of Italian women's feet has grown, this has now become a 37, equivalent to an English 4.

The last is then taken to a heel-maker, where the prototype is made: a mini sculpture either in MDF or plaster of Paris.

After the last has been approved, work begins on the model. The model maker, together with Sara, undertakes necessary modifications. It is at this point that that actual 'construction' of the shoe begins. The upper, which is the 'dress' that covers it, is cut out, and the sole and heel are made; in total, a hundred other single operations are required.

Not bad, for an object we walk all over!

International sizes

Salavatore Ferragamo divided women into three categories, according to their foot measurements: Cinderellas, Venuses and Aristocrats. Cinderellas were those with small feet, (continental 37s or US 6 and less); Venuses were exact 37s (US 6); while Aristocrats wore 38s (US 6.5 and over). The Venuses, blessed with perfect feet, according to Ferragamo, included the actress Susan Hayworth and the Duchess of Windsor, Wallis Simpson. Rita Hayworth was a Venus who wore a wide-fitting 37 (US 6A), while the extremely tall Greta Garbo was an Aristocratic 7AA, while Lauren Bacall, who had very long and wide feet, was a 9AAA.

When buying shoes abroad, one has to bear in mind certain differences in sizing. Here are some useful examples:

An Italian or French 37 is the same as an English 4 or an American 6.

An Italian or French 38 is the same as an English 5 or an American 6.5.

An Italian or French 39 is the same as an English 6 or an American 7. And so forth.

Epilogue

In the thriller *Blowfly*, whose central character is the detective Kay Scarpetta (whom we like everything about, including her name), Patricia Cornwell writes: 'Certain serial killers are obsessed with shoes and feet. There are men who get excited by particular types of shoes, and are overcome by the desire to kill their wearers. Many serial killers begin by stealing fetishistic objects, entering the houses of women and taking their shoes, underwear and objects that sexually excite them.'

It's enough to give you goosebumps. And it might even be true. Come on, girls, let's call a spade a spade here: would you give up your shoe collection for the abstract fear of a fetishistic killer? No, I thought not.

The biggest nightmare of a shoe-obsessed woman is actually quite different, and is perfectly depicted in a scene from the film *The War of the Roses*. In this, the husband, (Michael Douglas), in the throes of a messy divorce, picks up one of his wife's (Kathleen Turner) shoes, and saws off the heels! The exclusively male fear of castration doesn't even come near to it.

Thus, in conclusion, it is fair to assume that, if you have either bought or been given this book as a present, and you've read up to this point, you probably own a fair number of shoes. Or would like to. And you often feel guilty because it's never enough. And you often buy shoes that have nothing to do with either your lifestyle or clothes or physical type. Well, cheer up – you're part of a large tribe.

Joan Crawford admitted it: 'Shoes are my weakness.' And she confessed to owning three hundred pairs. Another Hollywood diva, Jayne Mansfield, owned two hundred. Two famous Eves in history were also shoe fanatics: Eva Braun, Adolf Hitler's mistress, and Eva Perón, the Argentinan First Lady.

A third, very famous Eve, Mrs 'Adam', is the only woman in history never to have experienced the fantastic thrill of choosing a pair of shoes. We feel for her. We understand why she got chummy with the serpent and how all hell broke loose. She must have been incandescent with rage upon learning that she was in an earthly paradise, without a single shoe shop in the neighbourhood.

Glossary

Pumps Round-toed shoes with a heel height of between nought and one and a half centimetres, inspired by the shoes of classical ballerinas, and patented in 1957 by Salvatore Ferragamo. These were made famous when worn by legendary actresses such as Audrey Hepburn and Brigitte Bardot.

Camparis Black patent-leather Mary Janes with a pointed toe and stiletto heel, an important model of the early nineties by the Spanish designer Manolo Blahnik, revered throughout the world by shoe fanatics.

Campers Round-toed, 'biscuit-shaped' Spanish shoes, loved by alternative, anti-globalisation youth throughout the world. Some models have a kind of split personality, with the left shoe decorated differently from the right.

Cinderella Protagonist of the much-loved fairy tale of the same name. Cinderella has to work as a skivvy, but in truth she is a girl of noble birth. A prince discovers this thanks to one detail, namely that she is the only girl in the realm who fits into a slipper, which in the Brothers Grimm and Charles Perrault version is made of glass. In the Chinese 'Cinderella' it is a golden shoe, while in Giovan Battista Basile's Neapolitan version it is silk. Whatever the case, 'Cinderella' is responsible for associating the shoe with the idea of a magic object, a kind of metaphor for femininity and fragility.

Chanel A strappy shoe that leaves the heel exposed, named after its creator, the legendary French designer Coco Chanel.

Cromwell A high-heeled shoe with a buckle in the front, which was very fashionable in England towards the end of the nineteenth century. The name derives from a mistaken belief that shoes with large buckles were worn during the time of Oliver Cromwell in seventeenth-century England.

Derby (or Oxford) Lace-up men's shoes (beloved also by many women), often two-toned (in this case, known as Spectators), which were particularly fashionable in the twenties and thirties.

Espadrilles Canvas summer shoes, of Spanish origin, with a rope sole. A flat version exists, which is often worn like a slipper, as well as platforms with laces up to the ankle. Most popular during the seventies.

Kruschev, Nikita Soviet politician who, during a fiery UN session, removed one of his shoes and banged it on the table. This story has got nothing to do with this book, but I mention it merely to draw attention to the fact that a woman would never dream of doing such a thing.

Marcos, Imelda Wife of the ex-dictator of the Philippines, Ferdinand Marcos, who was born in 1929. She was extremely wealthy, and famous for her outrageously lavish lifestyle. She was accused of owning three thousand pairs of shoes, a figure she always denied, claiming it was 'only' one thousand and sixty. A woman obsessed with shoes is known as an Imeldista.

Mary Janes American term for a round-toed strappy shoe, inspired by characters in an early twentieth-century comic strip, Buster Brown and his little sister Mary Jane. The characters' rights were acquired by the Brown Shoe Company, which, under the name Buster Brown, became the most famous American manufacturer of children's shoes.

Moretti, Nanni Italian film director, born in 1953 in Brunico, province of Bolzano. Well known for his obsession with shoes, particularly in the 1984 film *Bianca*, where there is a famous monologue on the subject: 'In the summer of . . . '72, I think it was, some women began to wear Dutch clogs, in white. Had they been to Holland? No idea, but all I know is that a couple of years later, all you could find were imitations: a higher heel, and these hideous metal studs . . . Though the black ones were nice, very plain-looking, a bit scuffed up. They were worn by girls with long blonde hair draped over their jumpers, dressed in blue drainpipes and red knee-high socks.'

Oxfords (see Derbys)

Penny loafers 'Loafers' or 'college' are an urban version of the moccasin. The name penny loafer derives from the habit, fashionable amongst American students in the fifties, of slipping a decorative penny into the front 'keeper' strap.

Sabot Generic French term for clog. In Italian it also refers to all slip-on shoes, be they high or low, which in English are known as mules.

Sabrina heel A kind of low, slightly curved, very feminine heel, inspired by Audrey Hepburn and by Billy Wilder's 1954 film, *Sabrina*.

Trainers All sports shoes, be they of the fashionable or technical variety.

Sperry top siders The first yachting shoe, as we know it today. This invention got its name from the American Paul Sperry (1895–1982). Born in Connecticut, he was a keen sailor who created an anti-slip rubber sole with zigzag grooves, inspired by the paws of Prince, his cocker spaniel.

Wedges Platform shoes, which were very fashionable during the Second World War, reappearing in different forms in successive decades.

Acknowledgements

My thanks to the people who have helped me in the writing of this book, in particular, Sara Porro, Fulvio Zendrini, Stefania Ricci and Mrs Wanda Ferragamo.

Thanks to Nicola Salerno for 'Elio's Song'.

Thanks to *Vanity Fair's* Editor in Chief, Carlo Verdelli, and Associate Editor, Christina Lucchini; but also to Enrica, Bombs, Tissy, Barbarina, and in general to all the editorial team at *Vanity Fair*, who have had to put up with me droning on about shoes for all these months.

Thanks to Maria Laura Giovagnini for daily moral support, as well as to my editor, Marcella Meciani, who, as they always say in these cases (though it's really true!), never stopped believing in me.

Thanks to my mother and all my girlfriends with whom I have shared many truly epic shoe moments over the last twenty years. From eighties cone heels to the bamboo clogs of 2002, from French pedicures to buying shoes on the Internet, it has to be said that we never wanted for anything, at least as far as our feet were concerned.

Special thanks to Gianmaria, for the (irresistible and comical) expression that he assumes each time I buy a new pair of shoes.

Last but not least, to Giulia Cogoli, who, apart from having many merits as a friend, introduced me to Marcella, Sara and Gianmaria.

A NOTE ON THE AUTHOR

Paola Jacobbi is a journalist and special correspondent for *Vanity Fair*. She lives in Milan.

A NOTE ON THE TRANSLATOR

Simonetta Wenkert's translation of *A Cercar La Bella Morte* (*In Search of a Glorious Death*) by Carlo Mazzantini was shortlisted for the *Independent* Foreign Fiction Award. She is the author of the novel *The Sunlit Stage*.

A NOTE ON THE ILLUSTRATOR

Emma Farrarons is a designer and illustrator. She was educated at the Edinburgh College of Art and l'Ecole Nationale Supérieure des Arts Décoratifs de Paris. She lives in London.

A NOTE ON THE TYPE

Guardi was designed by Reinhard Haus of Linotype in 1987. It was named after the Guardi brothers, Gianantonio and Francesco, the last famous artists from the Renaissance Venetian school of painting. It is based on the Venetian text styles of the fifteenth century. The influence of characters originally written with a feather can be seen in many aspects of this modern alphabet.